HUMAN BREEDING – THE ELEPHA

By Lyn Victor Williams

-

DEDICATION

I dedicate this book to my Mother and Father and my patient
Wife, my Son and Grandchildren, my brothers and also all my
neighbours and friends throughout my life who's company I
have enjoyed and, unbeknown to them, I have studied in my
own quiet way.

To the memory of my daughter, Rhysian & daughter-in-law
Dawn.

And a special thanks to my neighbour Ffion for help in
publishing.

PREFACE

I was born in the week that the second World War ended on a farm near Rhos, Pontardawe, South Wales. We, the family that is, left there when I was six years old and moved to the small village of Fforest Goch (Red Marsh) nearby. My father had started a family business as he no longer could do manual work due to an injury working underground. I had a wonderful and sensitive Mother to whom I owe a great deal, She always encouraged me to see the other person's point of view in any situation. I joined the family business when I left school at fifteen.

Meeting hundreds of people year after year got me interested in why different people were so 'different'. I often thought that if I could understand myself better it would help me understand others better. I have been interested in people ever since. I now feel that, hopefully, my experiences in life can help others. About five years ago it suddenly struck me that we are more or less controlled by our emotions. What triggered this thought was when I asked myself the question 'where do feelings come from when we feel them for the very first time'? The longer I thought about it and studied it in others, and myself, the more convinced I got that we are under their control – if we let them.

Let's get things clear from the start – I do not profess in any way to be an expert in any form of Psychology or Psychiatry, even though I've studied Humanities at University level for five years that only made me realize how little we know about ourselves. I don't pretend to be skilful as an author either, so please read the content of this book and not <u>how</u> it's written – no-one is good at everything! I hope you will find the writing refreshingly simple.

I avoid technical terms and quotes as much as possible, I'm not trying to prove or disprove anyone's theory, I'm just putting forward my own theories and observations, you must make up your own mind if you agree or disagree with all or some of them.

TABLE OF CONTENTS

Although I've studied myself and others around me, for over 50 years, I regard myself as an expert only in common sense. There is enough evidence to show that each generation is getting more stressed out than the last, turning to alcohol and drugs and sometimes even suicide because they don't understand how they are the way they are, and how others seem to cope and they can't. I find it very sad that more and more children, especially in America, are being treated with medication for depression and 'bi-polar' problems.

There are hundreds of theories in Psychiatry and Psychology that are very difficult to prove absolutely. Therefore 'experts' are reluctant to publish theories that have not passed extensive tests over a number of years, they are cautious and reluctant that if they do, the theory may later be accepted as being wrong, therefore, discrediting them and possibly affecting their employment prospects (I suspect it's the same in most fields). Progress, therefore, is very slow. Some experts, no doubt, think about very important theories which are common sense but these are either kept private or maybe, on the other hand, they are looking for complicated reasons for our behaviour and missing the obvious. Some very intelligent 'experts' lack basic 'common sense'. There are many good books with theories of where in the brain emotions come from, but none that I know of that try to explain 'how emotions get there in the first place'.

This book is designed to make you think about yourself and your feelings – question your emotions even when reading this book – self- awareness, to be aware of your feelings.

Most people look for an understanding of life – 'why are we here' - ' what's the object of it all' – perhaps turn to religion or a myriad of other things for guidance to try to find a meaning, a meaning to give themselves confidence that they will know what their purpose is in life. <u>I do not pretend to give all the answers to these questions in this book.</u> I believe it is up to the individual to find their own personal skills and exploit them. We often don't discover our natural skills 'til later in life- if at all, but I hope by reading this book more will find the answers for themselves and have a clearer picture.

What can be more important than understanding ourselves – enjoyment of life blossoms when we do because it makes us feel confident.

By understanding ourselves and why we behave the way we do we can understand others and hopefully create harmonious relationships, tolerance and forgiveness. One of the most difficult things in life is forgiveness- to forgive someone for a bad judgement against you or your family. Without forgiveness a relationship cannot prosper because the third party will always feel guilty about it and think that you hate them for it. But if they apologise in a genuine way and admit their mistake and you accept in a genuine way the relationship can still grow. I am not a religious person but I think forgiveness is a wonderful virtue to have, especially under the pressures that we live under to-day. Someone once famously said "to Err is to be human and to forgive is divine".

Perhaps we expect too much of ourselves – set too high a standard, one that we can't possibly achieve, we may then be disappointed with ourselves, feel inadequate or even depressed.

Understanding anything at all makes us feel more confident. It's difficult to enjoy life if we do not feel confident -confident with ourselves and confident with others, whether it be in work, at home, down the pub or in the gym. Relationships with others can be stressful. With every person we know we have a different kind of relationship – with one person we may behave in a totally different way than with another, whether it is with our spouse, friends or bosses and whether they are male or female. We may, to a point, want to create a different image of ourselves to each one. If we are in the company of all of them, the same time, it can get stressful, but by understanding ourselves it can be less stressful – we will know who we really are behind the 'facade'. Because everyone has a different personality/character, relationships are always going to be difficult. We consciously or sub-consciously compare ourselves with others in our social group. Where do we stand in the league table within this group. This may be a financial comparison (material goods) educational or moral/ethical standing. We may endeavour to improve ourselves within this group, in the category that is the most important to us, or just accept where we are and get on with life. It takes a lot of confidence to say to ourselves – 'well this is what I am and they will have to accept me as I am'. This may by O.K. in some groups but not others.

Do we have free will and control over our own lives or are our lives pre-programmed by our emotions? I believe we have innate animal instincts (feelings) and innate hereditary emotions, otherwise each generation would have to learn everything from scratch. If we depended totally on our feelings, and lived our lives by them, it could be argued that we did not have any influence on our lives because we are controlled by our feelings that are innate and therefore hereditary. We cannot, of course, go through life this way i.e. the boss would give us the sack because we would tell him/her what we feel about them. Therefore, I believe we must have a free thinking and independent brain that can question our feelings and keep our behaviour under control. Young children tend to be unruly because they go by their feelings/emotions because they haven't had any experiences in life to known any different and don't appreciate other people's point of view. It could be argued that we are born more animal than human but we must learn to be human to fit in to society.

BREEDING

After thousands of generations on our father's side and thousands of generations on our Mother's side of the family we end up with a single human being – you or I. That is the historical fact of every living human. And the more you think about it the more fascinating it becomes and explains why everyone is so different.

Whether we like it or not we can only be a percentage of our Mother and a percentage of our Father. Logically we cannot be anything else. They, of course, are percentages of thousands of others. If we'd had a different Mother or Father we would be a different person with different emotions passed down to us and therefore we'd have a different personality/character. Once the sperm meets the egg our fate is sealed and our <u>basic</u> personality/character is set purely because of a chance meeting of our parents, who happened to be in certain place at a certain time, we are who we are to-day. (Fascinating or what).

We would like to believe that we are true independent individuals, but this is not possible as we inherit most/all of our feelings and emotions from our parents (as is now generally accepted). These emotions will strengthen or weaken depending on the environment we are raised in. If we are raised in an aggressive environment and we have inherited an aggressive emotional attitude from our parent/s (which is likely) we will have difficulty in controlling this emotion and possibly not understand/like ourselves because of it – think perhaps that we have some kind of mental problem for behaving the way we do, perhaps different from others. If we speak to others, in depth (that we don't often do), we may find out that others have unwanted or extreme emotions too, but maybe control them better than we can and therefore seem perfectly 'normal'.

Siblings of the same sex can be so different in personality, skills and maybe looks, even though brought up in the same environment by the same parents. If exactly 50% of traits came from each parent then siblings would be exactly the same, like identical twins. So it's logical to assume that different percentages are at play at different times or that the joining of the egg and sperm is so complicated that it is inevitable that siblings will be different. Another reason would be that hereditary strengths and weaknesses may jump a generation (or two?) – more food for thought and study, but we cannot get away from the fact that they are hereditary.

Breeding, in regard to humans, is not a word we hear very often these days except perhaps in old British Empire or aristocracy films, for example. We usually hear the word in reference to race horses, cows or show dogs etc. But we breed these animals not only for speed, meat, size, colour or looks but also for temperament. If we want a vicious guard dog we would breed a vicious bitch with a vicious dog, for example. Alternatively we can treat a dog badly to make it vicous. We can, of course, also breed dogs that have pups that are placid or learn quickly (i.e. sheep dogs). Some dogs love the water and some don't because of generations of breeding.

Some, perhaps, may find it difficult to accept that there is such a thing as human breeding, is it because we don't like the idea of having so much influence on us through our parents/grandparents?

It could be argued perhaps, that domestic animal breeding can be an intentional mating, whereas human mating, usually, comes down to sexual attraction – nature's breeding programme. One person may find another person attractive and another person may not. I personally don't really know the answer to this one but if the belief that opposites attract is correct, it may be nature's way of ensuring that there is a continuing mix of different kinds of humans and perhaps also to ensure there's no inter-breeding! – evolution at work.

Is it arrogance that makes us believe that we are so different from other animals because we have a more intelligent brain? We have the same DNA but just arranged in a slightly different way. Are we in denial so that we don't want to accept the closeness to animals?

If we study an animal we can see that it has emotions too but whereby it relies totally on these emotions we have a logical brain to know when to control the 'poor' ones (most of the time) and when to use the 'good' ones depending on the situation. Animals, of course, can be trained to do things against their natural instincts, usually for a reward.

We hear comments like 'he's a natural at such and such a thing, but if we study the near relations of the person the 'natural' strength can be seen in them, weaknesses also can be seen. I used to believe that sons or daughters of sportsmen, for example, got on in the same sport because of their Father's or Mother's influence within that sport and not because they had inherited their parent's talent – I remember resenting them for it because they seemed to exploit their parent's contacts etc., my ignorance of course.

Because we are aware of our weaknesses we tend to be hard on ourselves because we are not 'perfect', but of course we should realize that no-one is perfect and everyone has some kind of weakness, some are better at covering up the weakness than others. But I believe that knowing the weaknesses are inherited will make people feel better about themselves, not get depressed about it and to concentrate on their strengths. Having said that, I don't think we really appreciate our strengths because they come so 'naturally' to us. Some may never realize them and some may realize them too late in life to exploit them.

Because each generation is in the process of evolving, each generation is at a different stage of development. We are evolving to fit into our present, but constantly changing, way of life which may be totally different from our parent's way of life. The pace of change is faster than evolution can keep up with. I believe we are still more animal than human at birth, and therefore must learn to be human (against our natural instincts) to fit into the particular society we are born into, a society that is constantly changing from generation to generation – no wonder we, and especially our children, get confused!

Each child is born with a different inherited level of confidence, which will grow or be subdued by the environment they grow up in, as stated. Most, if not all, feelings are inherited, we are not taught how to feel, they are in-built, and initially will live by these self- centred feelings and learn how to control them from the people who raise us – this may be consciously or subconsciously of course. We are taught only the names of these feelings and how perhaps <u>we should feel/behave in a particular situation</u>.

When I studied Humanities I wrote three papers because I felt the need to get my ideas down on paper and originally, when I first thought of writing this book, to integrate the three into the book, but later thought it would be better to print them separately, in their original state, and then adding a post script. Although some things within the essays are repetitive I do not apologize for this as I regard their context within each paper as important.

CONFIDENCE IS LIFE. (Paper no. 1.)

We can only enjoy life if we <u>feel</u> confident. The opposite of confidence is a feeling of hopelessness, being depressed, insecure and inadequate. The feeling of confidence makes us relax and feel good about ourselves. The feeling of confidence is good. We feel we are in charge of our lives – confident to try something new – to move on and up. If we feel we have wronged someone, or society, it reduces our confidence – will we be found out. But also guilt eats into our confidence – it's guilt that keeps most of us in line, we do not want to be knocked back morally in comparison to others around us. When we are guilty of an action we may make up poor excuses to make ourselves feel better, start a blame game perhaps or go into denial and pretend we do not care about others or what they think. Feelings can be a hindrance or an inspiration.

Confidence is a word I keep coming back to time and time again the more I think about life. Everything we do either lifts or knocks our confidence – depending on the outcome. Every person we meet, every conversation we have, either makes us feel better or worse about ourselves, consciously or sub-consciously. If we feel we are closer to someone, or we think we have impressed them, after a conversation with them it will make us feel good -if we think the other party thinks we are O.K. <u>we</u> will feel O.K. If we do well in a sport or a subject in school/college/work we feel more confident because we are better than most at it and we feel they respect us more, or perhaps it gives us a feeling of superiority . Confidence, of course, will rise and fall depending on how well we understand the situation we find ourselves in or the people we're with- do we understand what's going on around us.

It can be easy to lose short-term confidence if, for example, when in company we make a statement about someone or something but no-one else agrees or simply travelling to a town we visit fairly regularly we find they have a new one-way road system or we cannot find somewhere to park.

At an early age we are continually confronted with new challenges, if we do well in each, or most, hopefully encouraged by loving parents, we are able to move on eagerly to the next challenge. With each conquest our confidence grows. We are rewarded by our parents, verbally or otherwise, each time we are successful – this sets the foundation for our future and encourages us to improve continuously, helps us overcome fear of making a wrong decision. If we are successful in life, in comparison to others around us, our confidence keeps growing, but if we have a set-back to upset this pattern, illness say, injury, divorce or we make a big error of judgement that loses our credibility with others, this will knock us back down the confidence ladder. We then need to think positive and draw on our reserves of confidence to re-adjust and move on –treat it as an experience of life that we can learn from and feel positive that we have gained something from it.

But we, or our parents, may set too high a target for ourselves, targets we cannot reasonable achieve and therefore we are disappointed when we 'fail'. We need to set reasonable targets and try to achieve them in sensible steps. We are human and we therefore make mistakes, if we blame ourselves for every single thing that goes wrong in our lives it may shatter our confidence and make us feel inadequate and may even hate ourselves for it for being so 'stupid'. If we hate ourselves, obviously our confidence will be low and be unable to show positive emotions towards others – how can we love others when we don't ' love' ourselves and how can we expect others to love us. If there is no logical reason why we hate ourselves it maybe a poor emotion that we have inherited, but we can only change things if we are aware of them and what causes them. Poor emotions must be suppressed by positive logical thought. Total concentration shuts out poor emotions. "Know thyself –know your emotional state at all times", Socrates.

The thought of someone or something watching over us from above gives us a feeling of self- awareness and importance, this is why, I believe, religion is so important to so many people. The thought that someone or something else is partly responsible for control and guidance over our lives eases the personal emotional responsibility and gives confidence. The feeling of being totally in control of our own lives is a responsibility that many cannot cope with. Some people, of course, are more sensitive than others, some can cope with more pressure than others –feelings under control and in the right perspective.

We start life where everyone does everything for us, feed us, dress us, and entertain us- the whole world seems to revolve around us. But as we grow older we've got to learn the rules of the house and the rules of life as we move to independence and then the realisation that we have to start doing things for others. The process of moving from dependence to independence to the realization later of inter-dependence. We may be brought up into an environment where we get conflicting messages from our parents – different moral standards say. Mix into that our own feelings, it's no wonder there's confusion in our lives. But if we could have understood where our parents' feelings and our feelings came from, we could have followed what was going on. Our parents may, for our benefit, set high moral standards that we find difficult to live to, our feelings don't <u>feel</u> right. Confidence depends on how high or low we set our standards compared with the standards of those around us and what level we regard ourselves to be at in comparison.

As youngsters we do things to please others we love or respect, if we have the love of our family – we don't want to lose it, this keeps us in line. But if there's no one around us that encourages us and is prepared to listen to us, we will feel alone and not answerable to anyone and cannot see the point in behaving responsibly or getting on in life, it's easier not to. If we are not disciplined by our parents and not shown an example by them, we do what we want to do-rely on our own out-of-date feelings, we are in charge of our lives at too early a stage in growing up – this can be a frightening experience. We lose interest in what we are doing, because there's no one to share it with. We can't bear to be with our family because we feel they have let us down, or we have let them down, and by being in their company reminds us of this, it no doubt reminds them also, no confidence in the relationship, so we look elsewhere for attachments –that usually means on the street. There we are more likely to meet people of the same attitude – no respect for their parents or society. We turn to these individuals for some kind of relationship that we could not get at home, we are comfortable in their company. We may feel that we have to do things to impress the 'gang' to gain their respect. If their standards are low ours may need to be lower to be accepted – perhaps commit a more serious delinquent act or crime. Everything we do increases or decreases how we feel about ourselves within our group, increases or decreases our confidence within that group.

We obviously find it more difficult to be confident if we feel that others around us are 'better' than we are, better at sport, better in business or better looking. So we may strive to 'improve' ourselves (keep up) in the same areas or possibly in a totally different direction, if we know our own hereditary strengths, it depends on whom we are trying to impress –family perhaps or our circle of friends. I think this particularly true when we are teenagers to impress our friends, we want to be liked more, we want to show them we are just as good as they are or better, or if we are in the wrong company –as bad as they are. We cannot feel confident if we feel 'inferior'.

If we are brought up in an environment that is morally poor, perhaps embarrassed by our parents, we will find it more difficult to improve ourselves. We will find it difficult to break this cycle because in doing so we would possibly have to leave our 'friends' and family behind to move onto a higher rung on the ladder where we may or may not be accepted and possibly be rejected by our original 'friends'. Therefore it takes a lot of confidence to do this.

We are born with natural talents – it's our responsibility to explore life and find out what these talents are, whether they be physical or mental. Whatever the talent is we will improve at it because we are good at it and what we are good at we keep doing, it increases our confidence. On the other side of the coin, of course, we also should know our weaknesses and the danger is we will let them override our strengths and use them as an excuse not to do things, but we must realise that everyone has some weaknesses. We should either face up to these weaknesses, and accept them, or try to improve them. It's unfortunate, because it's so easy for us to do, we therefore don't appreciate the 'natural' talent we have.

Good relationships with others gives us confidence – it we feel we can turn to others when we have problems, it makes us feel good. But, of course, we must give others confidence too, listen to them, for the relationship to work. Confidence grows if our relationship with others, close to us, is O.K. – relatives, friends, work-mates, neighbours, fellow club members etc. Of course we will have a different kind of relationship with each person or group of persons. The key, I believe, to any good relationship is not to expect too much from others, we may be confident to-day but others, we may meet, are not and may be negative and depressed because things haven't gone their way. We go through periods of high and low confidence –if two confident people meet, it's O.K., if one is negative not O.K. If we are on the receiving end of a negative response it could make us depressed or upset and we possibly, if we are not careful, pass this on to someone else. It's difficult to understand when we are rebuffed but we should have the confidence to say to ourselves – he/she is having a bad moment, I'll speak to him/her later and not blame ourselves –not let it get us down. We must have the confidence to forgive others who have been negative or offensive towards us. If they think you are a forgiving person they are more likely to apologise and then the relationship can continue to grow.

We feel insecure when someone does not agree with our ideas on a particular subject. We like those around us to agree with everything we say but if we are confident we will agree to disagree,(if they don't), and move on, it won't seem that important. If we feel confident with ourselves we'll have more patience with others and listen to what they have to say without jumping in with our own presumptuous thoughts on the subject. To resolve friction between two parties, emotions must be put to one side and logical thinking must prevail to understand the other's point of view.

What's more important than what others think of us is what we 'feel' about ourselves. We can get away from other people but not from ourselves. We may behave badly in a way that no-one else would know about but 'we would know' and feel bad about ourselves – it would play on our conscience. Anything bad we do to others reduces our confidence – whether the other party knows about it or not – we would no longer feel comfortable in their company, perhaps subconsciously afraid that they 'may' find out.

We look for a meaning to our lives, thinking ourselves so important, something that's pre– planned - 'meant to be' – but there is no laid down plan. We must make our own plan – what do we want to do with our lives – where do we want to be in 5/10 years' time. We must plan and prioritise. We must have something to aim for. When things are 'going to plan' we are positive and confident, a sense of achievement. But how can we have a sense of achievement if we haven't achieved anything we have set out to do. When things are not going to plan, our confidence may wane and depending on circumstances, our frustration can make us do negative things. Our relationship with those close to us can became strained, we may feel we are letting them down or want to punish ourselves for making a bad mistake. The confidence scale swings to and fro but we must stick basically to our plan – if we don't have a plan we become part of someone else's plan. We must not let our emotions control us.

As children our parents take the responsibility of running our lives – life is O.K. –life is fun (most of the time). We depend on our parents to make all the important decisions and we just get on with our lives. As we mature we don't want to be dependent on our parents – we, naturally, want to be independent individuals, our own person, we may move out of the family home, to get married possibly, but we may still be in the habit of looking to someone or something to take responsibility for our lives, something to lean on – family perhaps or something to blame e.g. religion or government maybe, someone or something else to blame if things are not working out. It takes confidence to accept that we are responsible for our own lives, we must have a plan and make decisions for ourselves, whether they be right or wrong – it's so easy to fall into the blame game – my parents, teachers or bosses didn't understand me etc. and then don't do anything.

We will make mistakes in life – we must accept this and learn from them and move on. We are not usually content with ourselves because we know our weaknesses, we may look up to others – who seem to be perfect – but of course they have weaknesses also. Anyone of course who's looked up to by others, whether sports stars, film stars or religious leaders will find themselves under great pressure to keep up standards and not show their faults. It's a big responsibility to be responsible – living under the fear of being 'found out', so they often act irresponsibly to relieve the pressure, show others they are not perfect.

We are, of course, different things to different people, not just father, mother, husband, wife or friend but each person we meet we play out what we think they expect of us and perhaps depending on what their standing is in life. There's really few people we meet that we can by our 'genuine self'. We want to be liked by everyone because that gives us confidence, therefore, we act out our lives –different things to different people possibly – a charade. This can be stressful, the tension between what we feel we are and what others perceive us to be.

When we first meet a stranger, and whether consciously or subconsciously, it's like a kind of competition, who's the most intelligent, who had the best holiday this year etc., one trying to get the better of the other, our feelings may change with every sentence, depending on how controversial the subject.

Our confidence in a particular situation or conversation will fluctuate from minute to minute on whether we agree or understand what's going on, and of course who we are with. We balance our emotions with our logical thoughts –not easy on times. We are more confident, obviously, if our feelings and thoughts are on the same wave- length, no conflict. Our feelings are telling us it's right and we also have a logical backup if questioned on our opinion. <u>Confident we are confident that we are right</u>. On the rare occasion when we meet someone who's genuinely not interested in material things we would speak more about life, more about the basic things that we enjoy in life. Put our cheap materialistic emotions to one side – be relaxed.

If we respect each other as individuals and stop trying to get the upper hand on the other –respect the other person's position – we will have nothing to fear, we will get on with our lives without this fear of others being 'better' than us, losing out in the pecking order. If we' be ourselves' will we be more likely to gain respect of others?

We may think that we are the only ones that think a certain way and be afraid to talk about it. But when we <u>do</u> speak to someone, openly, we realise that others may think the same way and therefore both parties will feel more confident knowing this. If everyone around us, we feel, are on the same or similar level as us, there's no competition so we feel O.K. But if others in the group get on in life and we are not, we may feel insecure and lack confidence to 'not care'. Some, of course, choose to stay out of the competition and live a basic non-materialistic life, but we easily fall into to the trap of comparing ourselves with others. Some people haven't the talent to compete financially (if they want to), to boost their confidence, so they may try to be better at sport or just to be a 'better' person – helping others who are deprived or perhaps turning to religion for their confidence, being with people of the same mind-set. At the end of the day does it make us feel more confident – are we content within ourselves – are we achieving what we really want.

We tend, if we are not careful, put people into categories (stereotype), we think we then understand them. It's more difficult for us to accept the concept that everyone is different to different degrees, it makes life more complicated. We can also, of course, stereotype ourselves.

The difference between us and animals is that we have a thought process, We are not confined to feelings and visual memories and images only, as animals are, we can question our feelings and make decisions. Animals are in a more or less fixed routine, whereas humans can plan and make things happen. Positive actions to improve ourselves and not negative actions to knock others down

It's vitally important that we can show affection to others without the fear of rejection. We need to love others as we need them to love us, it gives a huge boost to our confidence. We love others and they love us. I cannot imagine a worst situation than that of a feeling of being alone in the world with no-one to love or be loved by. But how can we believe that someone else can love us if we don't have confidence in ourselves, to 'love' ourselves. We must have self- respect for this to happen. Love is appreciating and sharing your partner's strengths, but more importantly accepting their weaknesses. I'm alright with myself –you're alright with yourself. You know I'm alright with you – I know you're alright with me. <u>Confidence in each other.</u>

Feelings

Confidence is a feeling – we say we <u>feel</u> confident. But we also have scores of other feelings at different times in different situations that can affect this confidence. Love, hate, embarrassment, shame, guilt, apprehension, excitement, depression, elation, inferiority, sorrow, laughter, despair, helplessness, incompetent, lonely, superior, happy, inquisitive, frightened, etc.,etc. Frustration can build to such an unbearable pitch that the slightest thing may trigger an explosion of emotion totally out of all proportion to the situation.

So where do these feelings come from. Some believe that we learn them as we go through life and experience these feelings for ourselves from these experiences. I find this very difficult to believe. When you have a particular feeling for the first time – say guilt – you may not have seen anyone that looks guilty or the feeling 'explained' to you – you just' feel guilty'. It's already programmed into our hard-drive from birth – a hereditary feeling like all the other feelings we have. Our personality is our inherited emotions which may be introvert or extrovert. Many psychologists have studied identical twins separated at birth and all came to the conclusion that antisocial behaviour can be inherited. This confirms, in my opinion, that emotions/feelings are hereditary, after all even infants have personality/character. The depth of the different feelings could depend on our own experiences, if we've come across the feeling before, the strength of it may depend on how that original personal experience panned out, we may have a positive or a negative reaction. (our software).

So who do these feelings belong to? Most psychologists throughout the world now accept that 'some' key emotions are innate and therefore it follows that they are hereditary, but, I would say, why not all emotions. If we accept that feelings /emotions are hereditary then we have to accept that these feelings originally belonged to someone else – our parents/grandparents! If we are male do we inherit our Fathers' feelings, if we are female do we inherit our Mothers'?. We can only assume that we are a mixture of both otherwise we would be a clone, and siblings, of the same sex, would be the same in looks and behaviour. To evolve, do we inherit the strongest points of each of our parents. Do the strong points we inherit from our Mother over-ride the weaker equivalent points of our Father – evolution. Is it possible, as a male, to inherit our Mothers' sexual attraction, by accident, and not our Fathers'. Is

25

it possible to inherit both parents' feelings in the same emotion? Is it a wonder we get confused. Do all these inherited feelings apply in to-days world? Feelings that have been passed down for generations when our ancestors depended on their emotions to survive in the wild. Did inherited feelings and emotions help a son to fit into the occupational skills of his father, finding it easy to pick up the trade through muscle memory and feelings, assuming, of course, he didn't inherit his mother's feelings. If we accept this theory we would have to accept that no-one is a true individual – certainly not in early life.

If we study a child closely enough we can see traits/mannerisms of their parents in their actions and personality. I believe we can only be made up of a percentage of each of our parents, who are in turn a percentage of their parents etc. that is what makes us totally unique human beings, logically we cannot be anything else. Most of us, unfortunately, are burdened with some poor inherited emotions but of course being aware of them can help understand what's going on.

We are initially controlled by our feelings – any decision we make is firstly controlled by our feelings – no time to think. Our early ancestors couldn't think logically and therefore depended totally on these feelings and their own experiences in life. But when they learned to speak and therefore think they may have made a different decision by suppressing these feelings with their new found logic. If we are asked to make an important decision to-day, whether in work or in our private lives –say to sleep with someone, our emotions would firstly kick in and perhaps wanting it to be o.k., but when we logically think it through and the consequences of the act – what would our family think about it? – how will I feel afterwards? – the decision may not be so easy. Alcohol and drugs may have an influence when feelings may be more dominant over logical thought – false confidence.

We cannot separate our feelings from our thoughts. We cannot separate our thoughts from our feelings. Thoughts trigger feelings and feelings trigger thoughts. Sounds and visions (actual or imagined) can trigger either or both. If we see or visualise a certain difficult situation it can trigger an emotion that we can analyse by our thought process and make a logical decision. But it's all very well making a logical decision e.g. not to have that bar of chocolate, but our emotions may be far stronger and over-ride it. This is where we get confused within the conflict of logical thought and feelings. Because we have feelings that we don't like we may think there's something 'wrong' with us and perhaps mentally ill, but we should have the confidence to say to ourselves 'that's not what I want to feel – that's not my feeling' –keep control.

If we could resolve our problems purely by thinking, we could simply' think' ourselves out of problems. It would be easy to convince ourselves that bad things that happened in our past, were in the past and we can move on. It can be relatively easy to change our minds, but we cannot change our feelings so easily. If we could 'think' there's nothing wrong with our lives we would not question our lives, everything would be o.k. So if we are discontented with life it must be what we 'feel'. Day in day out we may 'feel' there's something missing in our lives –deep down we may know what it is but we may not face up to it, it's easier to leave well alone – less conflict.

We suppress some of our emotions because we 'think' they are selfish and that others may regard them as selfish. This suppression creates a conflict with what we feel we should do and what we 'think' we should do. It's this suppression that makes us frustrated – instead of doing what we feel we want to do we act out what we think we should do and what we think others expect us to do. If we just went along with our emotions we feel o.k. at the time, perhaps – but later feel guilty that we are thinking of ourselves before others. If it was possible to go through life doing exactly what we feel we want to, would we have any psychological problems? We are flooded with feelings of frustration because we feel we are doing or made to do things to satisfy others and not ourselves. We are afraid to lose the love or respect of others who we care about – afraid to upset them by letting them down – upsetting their life – insecurity for them. But if the truth were known perhaps they don't care particularly what we do – but it's what we feel about it that is important.

Whether we like it or not we do have feelings of selfishness. It would be totally unrealistic to think of others first in every given situation. We do things for others because it makes us feel good (selfish), we do things to increase our standing in society (selfish), we keep in with the boss (selfish), we keep our spouse happy –less aggravation or for reward (selfish), we suppress our natural feelings to fit in (selfish), we speak of altruism when we put others first, but it gives us a feeling of confidence/satisfaction that we've helped someone (selfish), we like others to think well of us and we're an o.k. person (selfish). Having said all this I still have a nagging feeling that there 'maybe' something deeper and natural that sometimes makes us altruistic. All I know is that it makes me feel good if I help someone. They are O.K. with me because I helped them and I'm confident that relationship with them is better.

We tend to look at life from our own experiences, feelings and thoughts, that others think and feel the way we do. This may be o.k. in some cases or may not. We think everyone else looks at everything the way we do and therefore act out our lives accordingly, thinking we're fitting in. If we keep suppressing our feelings do we end up with any feelings at all (nervous breakdown?) relying totally on our logical thoughts – will we end up not knowing who we really are.

Because of all this confusion we don't know our true self, is that why some take on a completely different personality/character, Napoleon say, delusions of grandeur, do they feel at least then they have only one personality to live with that's strong enough to block out the other mixed emotions? Others turn to religion or join a cult to clear up the confusing feelings they have and concentrate on a new purpose in life. Is this why psychologists encourage us to have a fixed plan in life so that we have a definite goal which over-rides other confusing emotions. Perhaps we all have these conflicting emotions but living in a positive, unstressed environment makes it easier to cope for some, but not others. .

I'm convinced we underestimate our hereditary feelings –which are in our inherited hard – drive, without them we couldn't have survived in the past if every generation had to learn everything from scratch. Added, of course, (as previously stated) to these feelings are our own feelings from our own experiences in life (software). But we must not underestimate our deep- rooted hereditary strengths and weaknesses. Is it possibly that these feelings are meant to fade as we grow older and our own feelings, from our own experiences, take over to adjust into the environment *we* find ourselves in? Are we constantly moving away from our inherited feelings to our own experienced feelings? Because of the environment of each generation is changing so quickly our hereditary emotions can't keep up – they don't fit in.

When someone seeks help from a psychologist they are usually confused because they do not really know who they really are. Conflicting emotions – inherited feelings telling him one thing (Freud's Id) and his shallow thoughts another (Freud's Ego). We can only cope with so many emotions at any one time (some people can cope with more than others) if we have inherited a mixture of personalities this will confuse our deeper logical thinking (Freud's Super – ego) that's trying to overcome the problem. <u>As stated we may be in a process of moving away from these inherited feelings into our own feelings, emotions and thoughts, but by doing so we have again this huge conflict between who we are "expected" to be and who we really want to be.</u> It takes a lot of confidence to be what we really want to be. Perhaps by speaking, in depth, to a psychologist it helps dismiss the negative emotions by facing up to them and not denying them. I believe we can only overcome some of our 'unwanted' hereditary emotions by facing up to them and then moving on.

Is it possible that hereditary emotions of both parents, especially of the mother during pregnancy, explain all or any of the following :-

A. Homosexuality – wrongly inherited sexual attraction from 'opposite' sex parent. Quote from New Scientist Magazine 21st. June '08. "Gay or straight, it's decided at birth" (or before?). Brain scans have provided the most compelling evidence yet that being gay or straight is down to biology rather than choice. Tantalisingly, the scans reveal that in gay people, key structures of the brain governing emotion, mood, anxiety and aggression resemble those in straight people of the opposite sex. "This is the most robust measure so far of cerebral differences between homosexual and heterosexual subjects," says Ivanka Savic, who conducted the study at the Karolinska Institute in Stockholm, Sweden.

B. Bi-polar. Two strong <u>inherited emotions</u> in conflict or battle between our own inherited feelings and our logical thoughts. A fight between our inherited character and what we really want to be or to appear to be to others.

C. Multi-personalities. Two or more inherited sets of emotions with movement between them.

D. Mood swings. Moving from one personality (set of feelings) to another depending on our level of confidence at that time.

E. Neurotic disorders. Instead of a conflict between the Id (feelings) and the ego (thoughts) is it a conflict between personalities within the person or a conflict between the Id and Ego within both personalities. Whichever the case the conscience (super-ego) must step in and make a decision. Anxiety is when we can't decide logically.

F. Emotional Instability. Confusing mix of hereditary feelings conflicting with our own. Uncertainty equals Anxiety. How can we be confident if we are unsure of our feelings? Feelings that trigger confusing thoughts.

G. Phobias. Inherited phobia feelings from parents or grandparents ? If there is no obvious previous personal experience to explain it.

H. Depression. One emotion pushing one way and a second emotion pushing another. Unable to logically decide so we shut down all our feelings to cope – can't see a way forward. If this happens in pregnancy is it passed onto the child? The child being burdened with poor emotions from its Mother.

I. Obsessive - compulsive. A gratification in an action that has no logical reason i.e. repetitive washing of hands. Again if it was a thought process we could easily change our thinking and easily rectify the problem. Again down to our inherited feelings which are stronger than our own common sense.

J. Schizophrenia – paranoia, delusion, hallucinations, controlled by spirits etc. when in one' personality' feeling the presents of a second 'personality.' Inherited mixed emotions.

K. Women who are pregnant in the winter months have more problem children (according to stats) and are more likely to be depressed in the cold, dark months before giving birth – emotions Mother passes onto the child before birth?

L. Do drugs and alcohol shut down certain parts of the brain, therefore, eliminating some of these mixed feelings so that we think/feel more clearly (right or wrong depending on quantity) – feel more confident? Is it our logical thinking losing control of our feelings.

M. Dreams. Are dreams a way of getting rid of the days frustrations or are they inherited feelings (perhaps parent's guilt) encouraging poor thought processes – nightmares?

We are nervous with people whose personality seems to be changing. We prefer people to stay as they are so that we think we understand them. But because we, and they, are in constant development towards our 'true' selves we both have to act out who we are expected to be. People who don't act out this drama are classed as eccentric or worse, because they do what they want to do, what their emotions tell them.. But is it that important that we have a personality façade or not, perhaps the important thing is that we know it's a façade and we know nearly everyone else is also acting out their life also to fit in?

Thoughts are our own – feelings are pre-programmed – but feelings trigger thoughts! If we think logically long enough can we change these inherited feelings that we don't really want or agree with. Would these new feelings be passed on to our children –evolution- after all birds and animals, in a changing environment, will change habits over a few generations to exploit the change – the one's that adapt the quickest will multiply the most.

If this theory is correct and we start off in life depending on hereditary emotions, and possibly replace them with our own, we must have the intelligence to be aware of them and control them. **To understand ourselves we must understand our feelings- to understand ourselves gives us confidence – CONFIDENCE TO LIVE OUR LIVES POSITIVELY.**

FEELINGS/EMOTIONS ARE OUR PAST – THOUGHTS OUR PRESENT AND FUTURE.
(Paper No.2.)

We are confused by what we don't understand. Do we understand ourselves.

When we understand how something works, a system or a piece of machinery say, we feel more confident with it. It's then logical to believe that if we understand what makes us tick, understand ourselves, then we will feel more confident within ourselves, understand what's going on.

What makes us behave the way we do?
What makes us feel the way we do?
What makes us think the way we do?
What makes us keep doing things although we logically know it's wrong e.g. gambling, where common sense is over-ridden by powerful emotions.
Feelings trigger thoughts – thoughts trigger feelings. 'Heart and Head'. Possible conflict between the emotional mind and logical mind – reasoning.

Why don't we all think the same way about everything or even the one thing. Some would say because we are raised differently in different environments, and this may be partly true, but I think it's deeper than this – I believe it's because we have different <u>emotions</u> about them, especially when we are young and without many life experiences to judge certain things by. If we didn't have different feelings about things everyone brought up in a similar environment would feel the same way about everything and therefore think the same way about everything until they experience something to the contrary or are told by someone, they respect, another way of looking at it which seems logical

THE BIG QUESTION IS WHERE DO FEELINGS COME FROM WHEN WE FEEL THEM FOR THE VERY FIRST TIME.

Feelings in our youth that we have not previously come across. Some believe we learn them as we go through life, but I cannot accept this – how can you learn a feeling from someone else or by experience. We don't learn feelings going through life, we only learn which ones are appropriate in a given situation and be able to put a name to them.

The human race would not evolve if we did not inherit some or most of our parent's/ancestors feelings/emotions–otherwise each person would have to start emotions afresh on a new learning process – on a blank slate. Humans had feelings and visions long before logical thought – to think we have to know a language and therefore mentally 'talk' to ourselves - that's why we feel first and then think second, thereby being in control of our emotions. We can also, of course, 'feel' other people's feelings although we may not have been in their situation ourselves, if they are sad their poor body language would indicate to us how we' think' they feel and therefore we feel a similar way in sympathy because we can imagine we are in their shoes. The strength of the feeling would depend on what sort of relationship we had with this person- how close we were to them and what sort of personality they had. A sensitive person may receive more sympathy.

If we accept that our feelings, emotions, instincts are hereditary, we are on the first step of understanding ourselves. We will

35

learn to suppress negative emotions and thoughts and get on with our lives – look at the good things about life and recognising good emotions and eliminating or suppressing poor ones –it might take some time to get into the habit, but we must persevere – we can't help our feelings, but we are responsible for them.

Common sense tells us that we should behave in a certain way so that we can get on with our fellow citizens but it may conflict with what we really 'feel 'we want to do – frustration. If our logical thinking and our emotions coincide we feel good, we feel O.K. If we are having a good day and everything is going our way, we feel relaxed and O.K., our feelings and our thoughts are in unison and therefore no conflict between them. Some people find meditation helps by shutting down emotions and eliminating thoughts and therefore no conflict. Poetry and music may also help, they can be inspiring or relaxing, again shutting out conflict between emotions and thoughts and encouraging confidence.

We all have inherited' basic' feelings – hunger, thirst, sexual attraction etc. standard <u>"Innate feelings"</u> we inherit to survive especially to fit into the environment we are born into, perhaps we should call them animal instincts that we need to survive our early years. We can see it to-day in children where the emotion of fairness is exceptionally strong – try giving one sweet to one child and two to another at the same time or the frustration when two children want the same toy to play with – a kind of self-preservation. <u>"Hereditary emotions"</u> on the other hand, are unique to us as individuals. But if we all inherited the same emotions <u>to the same degree </u>from our parents, siblings of the same parents would all have the same personality/character/temperament (which is not the case, of course). Different kinds of emotions are inherited to different degrees (I believe different percentages from each parent, maybe the strongest emotion from each one - evolution). Basic 'feelings' (animal instincts) may be the same for most but 'emotions' may be quite different. One sibling may be introvert and sensitive and another more extrovert and independent. Children live by their emotions/feelings, they seem wild and unruly-but they have to 'learn' how to behave within their society and live by the rules of that particular society/ family. Each and every family is at a different stage of change and development – evolution.

Basic Innate feelings (Genetic) **plus** Hereditary emotions (Unique) = an individual's character/personality.

A unique individual with emotions and feelings kept under conscious control by self- discipline (most of the time) by logical thought from personal experiences, parental discipline, born of necessity to ensure fitting into society/family life. We may treat others as we would like to be treated although this may be against our basic selfish instinct. We realise that we have to control some of our emotions and 'act out' our lives to different degrees. It's the fortunate ones that have feelings that are nearest to the way they actually 'want to behave' – the wider the gap between emotions and the way that we should act, the greater the internal conflict – wanting to act with our emotions but realising, reluctantly perhaps, we need to go along with our logical thoughts, therefore creating this conflict. Our primary reaction to any situation will be emotional, we will feel positive or negative toward it. Our secondary reaction will be to logically analyse the situation and our emotions (if we are patient and not react instantly) and see if our feelings correspond with the logical conclusion and 'then' react accordingly. We don't have to think or feel doing routine things in our own environment - feelings and thoughts have already been analysed previously, (which may be right or wrong) it's coming across situations for the first time, if we are wise, that we question our feelings and think through, and imagine the consequences – consequences to ourselves and others. Knowing how we feel at any given time and by accepting the feeling, we can change it or control it by logical thought – get it in the right perspective and to convince ourselves that it is the correct one. We lose our temper because we cannot control our emotions –cannot control the frustration. We should question each emotion we have, after thinking through whether it is appropriate to the situation we're in, then we can either go along with it or reject it. Our intelligent, independent brain, should control our decision –consider all the options and rely on cold logic rather than confused emotions that are either hereditary or our own feelings from our own (perhaps poor) experiences – our decision may depend on how it affects those around us, **but at least it's our decision.**

It's a huge responsibility to think that we are totally in charge of ourselves and believing that our hereditary emotions are initially controlling us, <u>if we let them</u>. But we should be intelligent enough to see this and use logical thought to make logical decisions to control them and act accordingly. We cannot change our sensitivity but if we are aware of its strengths and weaknesses we can control it. We may be dealt a poor hand as far as feelings go but that does not mean we cannot control them, <u>but first we must accept them – especially the poor ones.</u>

RECAP

BASIC INNATE FEELINGS. (Genetic)

Hunger, thirst, warmth, sleep, bodily functions, security, survival etc. These feelings can only be passed down to us from our parents – where else could they possibly come from? We must accept this as fact – we are not taught these feelings, they are built in. If we therefore accept this we have to accept that other feelings are passed down from parent to child – feelings that are not perhaps so basic and obvious and could be inappropriate for the way we live to-day. Males cannot inherit all their father's feelings/emotions otherwise they would be a clone, so the only explanation is that they inherit some of their Mother's. It's may be why we agree more times with one parent more than the other? Of course we cannot blame everything on our inherited feelings, we may be feeling tired through lack of sleep or depressed after alcohol, but we have to diagnose ourselves accordingly.

UNIQUE FAMILY HEREDITARY EMOTIONS.

Introvert, extrovert, insecurity, shyness, aggression – 'mental weaknesses'.(Schizophrenia, bi- Polar, depression)
It seems logical that males should inherit their father's feelings and female's their Mother's. Is this always the case? What if a male inherits his Mother's feelings, which could explain why some males act naturally in a feminine way – even explain why they are attracted to other males! When we are faced with a situation for the very first time the initial emotion we feel is natural – it's there already –built in to our nervous system. We are not taught how to feel – it's already there in our hard-drive – where else could feelings possibly come from? We can only be told by others if they are regarded as 'good' or 'bad' within that particular family or society. This may be different in other societies – adding to the confusion.

EMOTIONS FROM OUR OWN EXPERIENCES.

Previous experiences unique to us – these may be built in hereditary emotions but exaggerated by our own experiences of them. i.e. Previous poor relationships with the opposite sex. Anxious about making new friends. Fear of dogs from a previous incident or fear of failure in business.
Before we had language we depended on our feelings and emotions and of course our imagination (images) as our distant

ancestors did. We can solve a simple problem easily because we can imagine how to solve it pictorially. But a more complicated problem we may have to 'talk' through in our minds, talk to ourselves, to solve it.

To enjoy life we must feel confident – confident with ourselves and confidence with others. The opposite is a feeling of insecurity, questioning our ability and perhaps being depressed. If we can understand our feelings and emotions and control them, by positive thoughts, it will make us feel confident because we understand where they come from and we have them under control. We sometimes don't like ourselves, especially when we have aggressive or angry feelings, maybe for no apparent reason. It knocks our confidence because we are afraid that these emotions may get out of our control – the slightest thing might set them off, usually towards the nearest person to us, who may be completely innocent.

If we believe that we have poor emotions and therefore negative thoughts it's no good, of course, blaming our parents that we have acquired these from them –they've acquired them from their parents giving them, perhaps, poor negative experiences in their lives. So we may start off life with poor negative emotions, that we possibly can see in our parents. If we are fortunate to have positive, confident parents we may be lucky enough to have confident feelings to give us a good foundation in life. But it's no good feeling sorry for ourselves if we haven't, we must accept the situation and over-ride negative feelings with positive thoughts to then have positive feelings and get on with our lives.

If we accept the above theory as fact, how can it be useful in psychotherapy, psycho-analysis or psychiatry.

If a patient is having' psychological' treatment and having negative thoughts about life, feeling depressed or perhaps

40

having suicidal thoughts, for no apparent reason, would they feel a lot more comfortable with their lot if it was explained to them that these emotions are probably hereditary and not to think they are going insane or feel guilty about it. Would it help if it was explained to them that they had to learn to keep these inherited emotions under control by not reacting to them but to think things through logically, and have the confidence to act accordingly.

Emotion – Latin 'emovere'. Setting the mind in motion.

If there are doubts about this theory–the question needs to be asked again – **Where do we get emotions from that we feel for the very first time?**

A QUESTIONING OF PSYCHIATRY
(Paper No.3.)

One definition of Psychiatry –" Psychiatry is the medical speciality devoted to the study and treatment of mental disorders which include various affective, behavioural, cognitive and perceptual disorders, treatments include medication, psychotherapy and others including transcranial magnetic stimulation".

" Psychiatrists can counsel patients, prescribe medication, order laboratory tests, utilize neuroimaging in a research setting and conduct physical examination". National Institute of Mental Health (2006). Whether it be counselling or medication both will try to change the mental attitude that the patient has about himself/herself and try to remove or reduce poor thoughts, <u>as can street drugs and alcohol – temporarily.</u>

But I think they are barking up the wrong tree, when it comes to treatment, are they complicating the issue, innocently or intentionally. The word Psychiatry suggests psychic study – terms like mental problems, state of mind, mental disorder and mental illness, all suggest that all psychological problems are to do with the function of the brain – a mental breakdown or dysfunction. But should a 'Mental Status Examination' be called an '<u>Emotional</u> Status Examination'- is it a mental disorder or an emotional disorder. Perhaps nervous breakdown is actually nearer the mark-' state of emotion' and not 'state of mind'. It's easy to change our minds about negative thoughts but not so easy to change our 'feelings'. We can try to convince ourselves to be positive with logical thoughts but we may still have strong, negative feelings that keep coming back and haunting us, irrational feelings can over- power our common sense. It's stated that feelings come from a separate part of our brain called the Amygdala that in turn is connected to our nervous system, so when confronted with a potentially dangerous situation or a potentially very embarrassing situation our feelings will kick in first, whether we respond to these feelings or take a few seconds to think the alternatives through will depend on the circumstances e.g. A strange sound from within the house in the middle of the night.

We don't 'feel' like doing this or that, we don't 'feel' capable of doing a task, we don't 'feel' we can cope and may 'feel' we want to run away from the problem and we may 'feel' depressed. Feelings dictate our lives – if we let them. Feelings trigger thoughts (negative and positive) and of course thoughts trigger feelings. Negative feelings trigger negative thoughts- negative thoughts trigger negative feelings. If we remain in a negative state for any length of time, the danger is that we get 'used' to it and feel insecure when we have an opportunity to get out of it,' better the devil we know', so we stay in the negative – lack a feeling of confidence to get out of it.

The conflict between what we 'feel' like doing and what we 'think' we should be doing causes great stress and can become unbearable, and we may, due to the foreseen outcome, end up doing something we did not 'feel' like doing, especially in a work situation. This problem possibly added to many others we may already have. Perhaps that's when the nervous system shuts down (breakdown) so that we can cope and all emotions are switched off. I believe there are different kinds of 'thinking', visual planning (images), talking through in one's mind and also emotional thinking – how do I feel now before doing a task, how will I feel doing it and how will I feel after doing it. Also how I think others might feel about me and what I've done.

We may see an article advertised and feel we need to possess it but our logical thinking may try to over-ride the feelings because we can't really afford it, but the feelings may not go away so easily – we 'feel the need' for it – conflict between logical thought and feelings.

Animals and birds can do things their 'parents' did even though they've not seen it done i.e. Birds build nests, a certain breed of dogs will all behave in a particular way and we breed horses not only for racing but for the right temperament. Children go through stages of development like most animals do. Firstly being totally dependent on their parents for food, warmth and security etc. and then being able to do basic things themselves, feeding, toilet etc. -semi-independent. By the time they hit their teens they 'think' they are fully independent, it's not until later, of course, that most realize they are intra-dependant, their basic, perhaps inappropriate, feelings need self- control or controlled by others in the form of discipline. If we are lucky enough to be brought up in a family we respect we are more likely to have better self- control because we care about what our family thinks of us and we do not want to lose their love or upset them. If we don't care what our peers think of us we are more likely to go along with our own emotions/feelings because we haven't had perhaps an example to guide us any other way – we haven't had any personal experience in life to foresee the consequences of our actions or don't care and end up with social problems – no self- discipline.

Medication, drugs and alcohol alters the way we feel, therefore think, about ourselves -medication may suppress feelings and alcohol/drugs may give us false confidence but the point is that our feelings are changed. By changing the way we feel it may make us think more positive, but, on the down side, by being dependant on medication, or drugs or alcohol (subconsciously perhaps) cannot help our confidence as it takes away some of our independence and therefore our confidence – a vicious cycle.

I repeat, a number of psychologists seem to believe we learn emotions as we come across them in life ,but if that is the case how do we know how to feel when we come across a feeling for the very first time. Surely we cannot learn a feeling it must already be there before we can 'feel' it. We can only learn what the name is for the feeling. We not only see emotions in others – we feel them. We can't feel for another person unless we've already felt the emotion that the third party has, which may, or may not be from our own personal experience. We inherit physical strengths from our parents why not emotional strengths (and weaknesses). For mankind to evolve we need these inherited feelings for a good start in life, otherwise each generation would have to learn or be taught everything from scratch. We evolve over generations to cope with changing situations e.g. adjusting to city life from rural life.(or do we?)

In New Scientist Magazine 16/1/10 it states that it is generally accepted that there are Six Big basic emotions – joy, sadness, anger, fear, surprise and disgust. "the ones that everyone the world over exhibits- but we live in a more subtle world [to-day] in which other emotions have come to the fore. There are many contenders – avarice, embarrassment, boredom, depression, jealousy and love, for example, might epitomise the modern age". The article then goes on to explore five others that may be relevant – elevation, curiosity, gratitude, pride and confusion.

By studying other people and myself for most of my life I'm convinced that feelings/emotions are innate therefore inherited, if we observe youngsters closely we can see the mannerisms of their father or mother in them. Natural feelings i.e. Hunger, thirst, wanting to keep warm and fight or flight, for example, are innate feelings common to us all. Hereditary emotions,(modified slightly no doubt by each generation's circumstance- which some may be totally irrelevant in to-day's world) on the other hand are passed down to us through our parents from their parents – <u>whether we like it or not.</u> The strength of each depending on their initial primary 'levels' and the power of each will weaken or strengthen depending on our personal situation and experiences in life, especially the way we are treated by those around us. Our experiences in life will affect the way we feel about ourselves and about others. Why do some people cope better than others. Those who 'feel' confident will dismiss the negatives and carry on with their lives but those who let the negatives control their lives will have great difficulty in getting any satisfaction from life, but understanding where the negative emotions come from will give them confidence to think positive because they will understand themselves better.

Psychiatrists and psychotherapists should not be concentrating on 'Mental Disorders' but on 'Emotional Disorders' – as stated feelings trigger thoughts – good or bad. By going over the patients past is only part way to solving their problems, the patient needs to understand why they have negative feelings from their past and why they can't get rid of the negativity. Patients who think there's something 'wrong' with them mentally will be reassured that their problem is their 'poor feelings' and why they have them. If we can't understand our feelings we feel insecure and may even think we are going insane..

By examining a patient and discussing their case history a Psychiatrist or psychotherapists will try and alter this mental attitude. After several sessions the patient's attitude may change, but it's their feelings that are changing, feelings about themselves and the world around them. If Psychiatrists concentrated more on emotions, I believe, the patient will respond quicker and more positively because, after being explained where these poor feelings have come from (perhaps suicidal, homicidal even or other bad feelings) they would not feel so guilty. The understanding can be reassuring – getting the patient to understand themselves. Most patients improve simply because there's someone to talk to about these poor feelings and they feel someone cares – but if they understand where the poor feelings come from they would feel a lot better much quicker without the need for medication perhaps or any other further treatment.

If we accept that all emotions are hereditary, it's these emotions that should be analysed, which no doubt are stored in a certain part of the brain controlling the nervous system (or are they stored in the nervous system?). Why does one person feel one way about something and another person another way, when neither have experienced it before? it cannot be through personal experience so there must be inherited emotions at play. Is this what gives us different personalities? If we all felt the same way about everything we would all have the same mannerisms and personalities. Should Psychiatrists, therefore, be interviewing the parent/grandparents and questioning whether there's a family association of feelings? It's only fair to assume that we inherit some emotions/feelings from our mother and some from our father otherwise all siblings of the same sex would have identical characters. If this assumption is correct are we supposed to inherit the strongest traits from each of our parents – males inherit muscular strengths from their father and females maternal strengths from their mothers. Nature's way of improving each generation? But does this system sometimes go wrong, males inheriting sex drive from their mother and not their father and would logically explain homosexuality. There's no point in blaming our parents for our poor feelings, as they have inherited them themselves.

If we accept that emotions/feelings have a great influence on our actions do we have any free will? If we acted purely on our emotions the answer would have to be no. But we do not because logical thinking has to be in control e.g. Every day a certain percentage of people don't feel like going to work say, but of course they reluctantly do because they can logically calculate the consequences if they don't- keeping control of their emotions.

By having psychotherapy treatment on these lines would 'teach' our brains to suppress, or control these unwanted emotions – but we must first recognise them. Confidence plays a huge part in any treatment so if the patient can understand where their poor/negative emotions come from and being able to control them will boost their confidence so that they will have a positive attitude to look forward to a better and happier future
Not all poor emotions are hereditary, of course, fear of certain animals may be natural (for survival) but abnormal fear of everyday animals could be overcome by direct contact with the animal (familiarity) so the fear can be neutralised. But if it is a phobia or complex that is inherited it may not be so easy to dismiss. The fear of course could be from a passed traumatic 'personal' experience e.g. <u>Attacked</u> by a vicious dog, the depth of which could be so intense that it may possibly be passed on to the children without any vocal prompting from the parents..

Are dreams images from our inherited emotions? Many are studying why we have dreams/nightmares that we don't understand but if we inherit poor emotions could they be the trigger for them. Do feelings of insecurity trigger dreams. Research shows that children have bad dreams mostly about animals and as they grow older they dream less, is it because they understand more about what goes on around them- which animals are dangerous etc., therefore feel more confident and have more positive dreams and less nightmares. Does guilt make us dream negatively and therefore we wake up feeling negative. But correcting the cause of our guilt i.e. To apologise to someone perhaps, would rid us of the guilt and therefore dream more positive. If this theory is correct would it be more likely to keep us in line and less likely to do harm to others? Again it would be interesting to interview the parents/grandparents! Sleeping should relax us so that our nervous system can recover from all the emotions of the previous day and get them back in order. <u>Lack of sleep makes us loose our sensitivity</u>.

On studying the 'Index of Psychiatric Disorders' through from Anxiety Disorders to Voyeivism, phobias, panic attacks and obsessions most if not all could be explained/argued because of poor inherited feelings/emotions, no doubt in some/most cases exaggerated by their social upbringing. Being born with depressing feelings would not help growing up in a home of depressed people.

Some turn to meditation where they try to turn off their emotions and their thought process in an attempt to nullify the conflict between the both.

This conflict between logical thought and feelings will make us turn perhaps to someone or something for reassurance or maybe something we're good at to give us confidence so that we can think/feel more positive about ourselves. Some, of course, turn to religion for this confidence if they believe this will help them make sense of things, others of course turn to alcohol or drugs.

So should psychiatrists/psychoanalysts be called <u>Emotionologists!!</u> I believe that the problem is more biological than psychological or psychiatric.

I believe the conflict between logical thinking and emotions is the root of most 'psychological' problems. Is this theory so obvious that it has been overlooked by 'experts' looking for more complicated reasons – do psychologists and/or psychiatrists know this theory but are afraid to raise their heads above the parapet?

This theory I believe can explain so many things that are regarded as 'psychological'.

As someone once famously said "He who conquers himself is the greatest warrior".

That concludes my three essays, I would now like to share with you my general thoughts on the above.

DENIAL OR SELF DECEPTION

To help us to cope we sometimes blot out some thoughts that are most probably triggered by poor feelings, but if we know where the poor feelings come from, and why, we can face up to them and control them – we can control things that we can understand, in control of ourselves.

If we are not sensitively aware of our feelings is it that we cannot face up to them, therefore ignore them – a kind of self-deception, or perhaps selective memory. It takes will power to keep emotions under the control of common sense – common sense is obstructed by emotion, a kind of denial?

PREJUDICE

Prejudice is an emotion of insecurity and lack of confidence in ourselves, anyone we don't understand is felt as a threat. Fear of the unknown and unable or not wanting to see others point of view or belief and accepting that they may be different from us. We are nervous of others that we feel do not think or act the same way as we do, i.e. different religion or nationals or even different social class, that we don't know much about. Who's to say who's' right' or 'wrong'. Negative stereo-typing can lead to prejudice and possibly outright discrimination.

We don't need to analyse whether we like someone or something – we can feel it, that feeling of course could be 'wrong'.

We have natural feelings of negativity towards strangers or someone who's different from us. But we are naturally attracted to someone who we think is similar to us - 'Birds of the Feather'- it could be classed as a mild prejudice but I believe it's nature's way of ensuring that similar people actually multiply and there remains a high percentage of different kinds of' groups of people' –nature's way of keeping balance.

By being able to see the other person's perspective, even though they may be 'different' from us, reduces intolerance and makes us more altruistic and makes them seem less of a threat.

As someone once wisely said – "The only way to have the right attitude is to know what the wrong ones are and how you got them and why we keep them".

PERSONALITY AND CHARACTER.

Our personality and character is based on the conflict between our inherited emotions and who we really want to be and who we really want to be seen to be. We talk of the soul, our personality, our character or temperament, all these, I believe, are tied up in the battle between our emotions and logical thought.

DEPRESSION.

A dictionary explanation for depression – "a poor state of mind". I would question this as it should read 'a poor state of emotion' or 'a poor state of mind caused by a poor emotional state'.

We tend to feel anxious when we don't understand what's going on around us, it applies also when we have feelings we don't understand or don't want, we get confused which can lead to a lack of confidence and feeling depressed.

Some emotions can hit us instantly, of course, for example if we hear of a sudden death of someone close to us. This kind of news can lead to a relatively short period of time being depressed or maybe longer depending on circumstances and possibly the consequences of the death, perhaps a feeling of regret or remorse, for something that happened between us in the past which can eat away at us. But being depressed after this kind of news we can understand and perhaps we'd feel guilty if we didn't. We may also feel consoled by the sympathy of others.

We have an odd satisfaction when others make mistakes as long as the outcome does not affect us! Is it because we constantly, consciously or sub-consciously, compare ourselves to others and sometimes feel inadequate when it seems that others are improving their standard of living say, but when they slip back we feel this mild satisfaction, perhaps with a touch of guilt because we feel that way. The kind of relationship between us and them is of course important on how we would react. **BUT DO WE EXPECT TOO MUCH FROM OURSELVES – SET TOO HIGH A STANDARD THAT WE REALISTICLY CANNOT ACHIEVE?** We encourage and perhaps pressurize children to be better at education and sport say, but if they fail they feel they are not 'good enough' or have let others down and therefore get depressed. By this kind of encouragement we put children under immense pressure. They must be educated to the fact that they cannot be good at everything, some children are good at some things and not others. The important thing is that they understand that whatever they're good or bad at those around them will still love them.

If we are depressed we must firstly be aware that we are depressed, which may not always be obvious to us if we are in that frame of' mind'. If we are aware of it we can work our way out of it with logical thought, figure out why we have this depressed feeling or if there is a history of depression in the family at least we know why we are depressed and work harder to overcome it –easier said than done perhaps. But at least we will know why!

Do we expect too much from others. The feeling of pressure when others look up to them with respect or for guidance or just in awe. Pop stars, actors, sporting stars, religious leaders, for example, must find it hard to keep up images and perhaps moral standards, afraid to let them slip. I believe that is why so many act irresponsibly so, therefore, no-one expects them to behave in a responsible manner therefore taking pressure off them. They may feel this prevents them from getting into a depressed state or of course they just do it deliberately for the publicity, depending on their occupation and personality.

When depressed we may turn to over-eating –more common for women, or over-drinking – more common in men. Some find buying new things an anti-dote, all may lead to further depression i.e. putting on weight, the after- effect of alcohol or potential loss of finance that we really could not afford, in buying things we really could have done without. Alcohol and drugs, of course, change our general feelings, for a short time, we felt O.K. during that period, giving us false confidence and suppressing our frustration and taking us away from reality. Some might find this O.K. but only if it does not develop into a habit of regular heavy drinking which can lead to more problems and further depression.

We naturally feel more depressed in a dark room which has no lights or dim lights, that is why it is recommended to be in a bright environment and preferably with positive thinking people.

MORAL STANDARDS.

If we accept that emotions are hereditary, as stated, then it is fair to accept that it is an evolutionary process. For us to evolve we must change to suit our environment – as life changes we must also change to survive. The problem is that society has changed at such a fast rate in just a few generations that emotional evolution cannot keep up and therefore left behind – the process being too slow to adjust. For hundreds of generations general society changed very gradually, giving each generation a chance to cope with minor changes over a long period of time. It would change, of course, at different rates in different parts of the country. Years ago moral attitudes and new ideas may have started say in London but taken months, years or even generations to spread throughout the country. To-day, for better or for worse, they change practically daily because of modern technology and the media. We then face the constant conflict of moral standards that are continually changing. Youths, especially to-day, need an example of moral standards from those around them (especially parents). They look up to people in entertainment and sport (celebrity culture) but who may have poor moral standards. People with high moral standards are usually regarded as boring.

It's difficult to keep high moral standards that are constantly being tested by the rest of society. We are constantly being bombarded on television, for example, by poor ethical standards. Their aim is to be controversial therefore morally poor.

Where can the standards for moral behaviour come from?. Who should set these standards – do we need a new code of ethics to live by. Should they be set by religious authors? Politicians? And who should appoint them? Should self- respect set the individual's moral standards? We are born innocent, we have not offended anyone or behaved illegally or immorally, so therefore our moral standards are set and judged by those around us and combined with our inherited emotions. But their standards may be very high and we may find it difficult to keep up with them, we may rebel when we get older or persevere because we have respect for our parents –not wanting to offend them. If we set our own moral standards we must take responsibility for them and answer to the consequences, it could be easier to go along with other people's standards. We should be intelligent enough to foresee how we are going to 'feel' after we have made a particular judgement – what will we think of ourselves, and what will others think of us afterwards – self-respect. If we respect ourselves we also will gain the respect of others who also have good moral standards. If those around us have poor morals this, of course, can be more difficult, but not impossible. A child with poor emotions and morals that's moved to a 'better family environment' may be able to cope better with their emotions but the underlying problems may still remain but now easier to control. We must not be slaves to our inherited emotions.

ANIMALS.

We are known as a nation of animal overs. Why do we feel such affection for them? One explanation is of course that animals depend on their emotions only and there is no devious plan behind the affectionate feelings they show as there maybe with another human. We, obviously, show affection towards animals which can be therapeutic, generally without the fear of rejection. Rejection by another person can be very hurtful. Animals, of course, depend totally on their instincts/emotions and what has previously happened in the same situation before, by a series of images. They too of course inherit strengths and weaknesses i.e. some breeds of dog love the water and others don't, some horses are bred for speed and others are bred for looks and temperament (emotional response).

We all, of course, still have animal instincts which can get us into trouble e.g. sexual attraction, especially after alcohol, that changes our emotional state – behave in a way we may regret later.

ALCOHOL AND DRUGS.

It is an increasing worry that youngsters 'feel the need' to drink alcohol to excess (or take drugs) is it caused by the feeling of frustration, a way of reducing this feeling, or is it just camaraderie, showing how much they can drink and therefore be part of the gang- have a good laugh, sometimes at others' expense. I believe that it's most probably a combination of the both. The biggest worry is that alcohol by most seems to be accepted as a way of life, the norm, and teenagers are expected to behave like drunken yobs. Unfortunately the only ones that gain from this attitude are the drug dealers and the breweries.

So where does this feeling of frustration come from. Some no doubt feel that they have no future, perhaps they've had a poor education (maybe their own fault, but now regretted) and therefore only 'live for to-day'- what's the point of planning for the future, they'll only be disappointed, setting their ambitions far too low. The feeling of frustration, of course, may be caused by inherited poor emotions and being raised in a frustrated environment at home and therefore leading to poor confidence. At least one study shows that sons of alcoholics are more prone to anxiety and stress but get a bigger relief from drugs and alcohol – more so than others. It is imperative therefore that these youngsters (sons of alcoholics) are made aware, early on in their lives, that they are likely to have this problem and hopefully seek help.

EDUCATION.

As part of our education curriculum should children be taught how to respond to different emotional states within themselves and spot emotional states in others. When child a. is angry with child b. child b. needs to understand that it's not necessarily that child a. is angry with them 'directly' but the frustration in child a. explodes against them because of something or someone else, but they happen to be in the firing line. Should children be taught how to recognize their feelings, understand what they mean and how to react to that feeling. Try to understand that others have emotions too and therefore understand better their point of view. There would be no need for a separate lesson for this, it could be incorporated in the first class of the day where each child would state how they felt that day. The teacher and the other pupils could then pick-up each individuals emotional state that day. If the same pupils had negative responses day after day the teacher could perhaps speak to the child separately from the class and hopefully reassure the child, find out whether it's a school problem or a home problem. After all this could be the most important time of their lives.

A good education gives a child more confidence, therefore, more self- control and less frustration when they compare themselves with others. More self- respect to look after themselves and therefore more confidence to understand others and more confidence that they'll get on in life.

GROUP RELATIONSHIPS.

 Most of us feel the need to be part of a family group. But the larger the number of people working/living close together i.e. large town/city or large office, the more impersonal the environment is, harder to be respected as an individual and people generally come and go and therefore no time to form any kind of close relationship, be afraid to have any kind of relationship because they will more on. In a small community or work place closer relationships can be formed making us feel more important within the group – less frustration and inner anger. We get to know about other people's personnel problems and feel we can tell them about ours – natural therapy. We need to be loved by others but also we need to love other people without the fear of rejection.

Within a close group if someone is depressed or grieving or elated even, it tends to spread through the whole group. We share the other persons' sad feelings in empathy or we feel happy also if they are. We are generally good at recognising other's feelings but the way we respond will depend on what feelings we already have for that person or what has happened between us in the past. It is important also how we feel in ourselves at that particular moment, we may be in an anxious state with our own problems or may be late for an appointment and not show any sympathy – which we may regret later. The strength of our empathy will ebb and flow – It's difficult to be empathetic to others when we have so many 'problems' ourselves, you want to tell others your problems not listen to theirs. We can only cope with so many things on our mind at any one time. We may be able to cope with a few problems but that extra problem, which may be trivial in relation to the others, will send our nervous system into an 'unable to cope' mode – common sense goes out the window. We may stay in this stressed state until we can get rid of some or all of these problems or we can gather our thoughts and get things in perspective and chill out, this is not easy to do when we're stressed but being aware of our emotions is a major step towards controlling them.

A group of people who have successfully achieved something of importance or who worked through a potentially dangerous situation, have a certain camaraderie, a feeling of being part of a close group and that they don't have to prove anything to each other, a mutual respect which of course happens in team sports. A question of how do we feel about others and how do we think they feel about us.

INDIVIDUAL RELATIONSHIPS.

I think the most difficult kind of relationship is between two people, especially if they live in the same house, complicated further if others live in the house also. Each person is in a different emotional state at different times. Each having different inherited emotions, that strengthen and weaken depending on circumstances at that particular time. It's important, if the relationship is strained, that both parties talk about their emotional state so that both parties can try to understand where the other is coming from. A comment made by one could receive a negative or a positive reaction from the other possibly from their out-of-date feelings or maybe manage to keep their emotions under control and give a more reasoned reply. If we've had a really bad day and every decision we've made seems to be the wrong one, this can obviously knock our confidence. When arriving home the frustration can explode onto other innocent parties or we feel inadequate within the relationship – we're not good enough, that can also strain the relationship.

If the relationship has deteriorated so far that one or both parties don't even try to understand the other's point of view or try to compromise, it will be a difficult place to come back from – wanting the relationship to work is 90% of the battle – allowances have to be made by both parties, allowances on how we want to behave and how we should behave – no-one is perfect.

Within a group, or with our spouse, we are expected to behave in a certain way, perceived expectations, whether club mates, workmates or family members this can add stress to the individual to play out what's expected.

The way we feel about specific things, or in general, we assume everyone else (at least of the same sex) feels the same way. But with experience in life we realize this is not the case. Different situations may be taken differently by different people – different emotional response.

When we are alone with our own thoughts and feelings we are relaxed as there is no need to act out any facade to anyone – we can be ourselves. But we tend to act differently in the company of our spouse, neighbour or a total stranger – we are a different person to each one to a certain degree. Relationships with others changes continually, if we have not spoken to our partner all day, when we meet we would react differently than if we had only been apart for ½ and hour. If we had not seen a friend for a number of years our emotional reaction would again be different to someone we had seen every day. Good feelings can lead to good relationships but we must also appreciate that other's emotions are also changing.

FOOD FOR THOUGHT.

As previously stated more and more feelings, emotions and instincts are being accepted throughout the world as being innate – happiness, sadness, fear, anger, surprise and disgust, common in all kinds of civilizations from Australian Aborigines, the tribes of Borneo to Eskimos. Some argue that all other emotions can be covered by the above headings, I believe that all emotions are innate. Identical twins separated at birth will grow to have the same temperament (emotions). Innate means built – in at birth therefore must be accepted as being hereditary. The strength of some of these being out-of-date, they helped us survive for thousands of generations but may not be appropriate to-day. I cannot believe that we all inherit feeling of the same strength i.e. anger and fear will be stronger in some than in others. I believe that is why we are all different in character and personality and a mixture of our parents and their parents – whether we like it or not. If this was not the case everyone brought up in a similar environment would act and feel exactly the same, from personal experience we know this is not true. Two brothers can have totally different personalities – a mixture of their parents' DNA. What ratio may depend on the strength in each parent of a particular feeling, the strongest may dominate in the child, evolution. Our own experiences in life will strengthen or weaken these basic inherited emotions, being raise in a' good' family environment may keep' bad' feelings under control.

The out-of-date feelings often give us the wrong signals. Any situation that we are confronted with, we feel first (gut feeling) and either act instantly on the feeling or quickly think it through, perhaps reducing the strength of the feeling, then respond – depending on the circumstances. We may respond instantly to a friend perhaps but more 'thoughtfully' to our boss.

We are, most of the time, in conflict with ourselves to different degrees, depending on our life situation and the number of problems we have at that particular time. We may already feel frustrated with feelings of wanting to do one thing and our logical thinking another. A family man wanting to go to the pub or a football match, say, may be torn between his family responsibilities and his emotions. He may be feeling fed up with his job, but thinking logically, sticking it out for the sake of finance for his family, or something might happen in work and in the heat of the moment tell the boss where to stick his job – emotions out of control. Perhaps emotionally regretted afterwards. Some emotions can be dormant but triggered in certain situations.

We may also feel comfortable in our own little world when things are going O.K. (regular routine) perhaps can't face the emotions of change. There are things we know we should do but keep putting them off, we need confidence to accept change.

It's a good thing to think positive to convince ourselves to feel positive. Being positive about ourselves makes us look after ourselves better. Eat more healthily, be more hygienic, exercise more etc. because we care about ourselves – be more confident. Why do we sometimes feel depressed? We must analyse what we're not happy about in life, although we may not be able to do anything about some of them but at least we'll know why we're depressed and correct the things that we can do something about. Perhaps just concentrate on one thing at a time and sort it out. When depressed we might wanted to be left alone, but being with company could lift us out of it, no good sitting for hours watching T.V. we need to get out into the real world. It may be that we can explain why we are depressed and negative, lack of sleep say, but if we cannot explain why that is then we should turn to our inherited emotions for an explanation.

As previously stated this theory is not meant to clear our conscience of guilt by blaming our parents for our poor emotions but to understand where they come from and control them.

If we did not think and plan things through we would just be another animal. We are, most probably, the only animal to be aware of our emotions (self- awareness). We need to analyse our emotions as they arise, of course, we do not need to analyse every emotion every time we come across them – we have already analysed most of them previously, rightly or wrongly, and therefore do not need to check them again. If we did we would use up unnecessary energy through the constant need of balancing between feelings and logical thought. Only emotions in certain situations that we have not previously come across that we need to analyse and act upon with logical reasoning. If our decision is correct no further thought is required, but if questioned by others, or ourselves later, a further appraisal would be needed and hopefully a correct prognosis for next time we come across the problem, if we don't we will stick stubbornly to a wrong analysis, perhaps not wanting to, or can't face up to it.
If we lose control of our emotions occasionally, depending to what extent, usually no harm is done, but if we let our emotions take control we may only be able to cope by shutting down our emotions completely – a nervous shut down.

Emotional awareness comes from experiencing different situations in our lives. By reading this book I hope that the process can be speeded up and readers can understand themselves better and live a longer portion of their lives in contentment.

SUMMARY & SOME FINAL THOUGHTS

I started this book by referring to human breeding and the inherited emotions passed down to us through thousands of generations' emotions on both sides of our parent's families that makes us who we are to-day. Our own experiences and traumas, of course, are also added into the emotional mix. When I first thought through this 'theory' I felt a bit uncomfortable about it, but once I faced up to it I felt a sense of relief as it could explain so many things (N.B. I didn't want to believe it just to explain my poor behaviour in the past). Why I behaved, or wanted to behave, in any situation or relationship now made sense. Why did it seem that I wanted to react differently from other people in that same situation. It's possibly, of course, that they felt the same as I did but kept it under control and to themselves.

I believe that to understand ourselves we must accept the concept of Human Breeding and its emotions and how we must not be controlled by them but must learn to restrain them with patient logical thinking – thought before action. We must learn to question every instinct, feeling and emotion we have and whether it is appropriate for the situation we find ourselves in, whether it's relationships, that generate strong reactions, or any decision we have to make. As stated earlier in the book, alcohol and drugs can change our emotions and the ability to control them. Because each one of us is different, to different degrees, we must find our own way of achieving control –meditation possibly, exercise or perhaps to just understand that everyone else is going through similar stresses.

What would be regarded as 'Normal' in a psychological sense? Because we are all different it is difficult to define 'Normal'. But I would say that normal is the ability to control our 'out of date' emotions/feelings. Therefore, logically, abnormal would be the inability to control them and let them take over our every decision (perhaps only some/most of them).

If there's no obvious reason why someone has 'psychological problems' i.e. poor or difficult upbringing or personal trauma, it makes logical sense to me that if they are taught that their problems are from inherited emotions they would understand themselves better and react to treatment much quicker or even sort themselves out. But the person must, of course, want to understand and want to be 'better' – not being held back by depressing emotions, for example, that may be inherited anyway.

I wonder why psychologists and psychiatrists don't comment anywhere, at least anywhere I could find, about this subject as a treatment method. Is it so obvious to them that they think it's common sense and everyone else knows about it, or is it because if they did refer to it that they would be accused of being elitist or upper class and maybe do themselves out of a carrier, or is it because they think that the general public would not be able to understand or cope with this, they think perhaps, unnerving knowledge. If the latter is the case I don't think it is their responsibility to keep it hidden and that they underestimate the intelligence of the general public.

Whether I've convinced you or not about human breeding I hope it's made you think about yourself and made you more aware of yourself. If I've helped a few people along the way who thought they had 'psychological problems', my ambition has been fulfilled.

6082407R00038

Printed in Great Britain
by Amazon.co.uk, Ltd.,
Marston Gate.